NUMBER ART

upper left: Armenian; *upper right:* Tibetan; *lower left:* Thai; *lower right:* Chinese

NUMBER ART

Thirteen 123s from around the world

WRITTEN AND ILLUSTRATED BY

LEONARD EVERETT FISHER

FOUR WINDS PRESS   NEW YORK

SPECIAL ACKNOWLEDGMENTS

To my wife, Margery M. Fisher, Librarian, Coleytown Junior High School, Westport, Connecticut, a constant mathematician without whose concept and resources neither this volume, *Number Art*, nor its predecessor, *Alphabet Art*, could have happened.

To Sylva N. Manoogian, Principal Librarian, Foreign Language Department, Los Angeles Public Library, Los Angeles, California, who provided me with rare assistance and expertise.

To Thea Langseth, College of Education, University of Minnesota, Minneapolis, Minnesota, whose special research was timely and invaluable.

LIBRARY OF CONGRESS CATALOGING IN PUBLICATION DATA

Fisher, Leonard Everett.
  Number art: thirteen 123s from around the world.

  Summary: Traces the development of the various number systems that have been used in the world, including the Arabic, Chinese, Egyptian, Gothic, Greek, Roman, and Sanskrit systems.
  1. Grammar, Comparative and general—Numerals—Juvenile literature. [1. Number systems. 2. Numerals]
  I. Title.
  P275.F57   415   82-5050
  ISBN 0-590-07810-0   AACR2

NUMBER ART

CUNEIFORM Babylonia c.3500 B.C.	HIEROGLYPHIC Egypt c. 3000 B.C.	LINEAR B Crete Mycenae c. 1500 B.C.	ATTIC Greece c. 400 B.C.	ARABIC Modern European	CUNEIFORM Babylonia c.3500 B.C.	HIEROGLYPHIC Egypt c. 3000 B.C.	LINEAR B Crete Mycenae c. 1500 B.C.	ATTIC Greece c. 400 B.C.	ARABIC Modern European
				ZERO 0					SIXTY 60
				ONE 1					SEVENTY 70
				TWO 2					EIGHTY 80
				THREE 3					NINETY 90
				FOUR 4					ONE HUNDRED 100
				FIVE 5					TWO HUNDRED 200
				SIX 6					THREE HUNDRED 300
				SEVEN 7					FOUR HUNDRED 400
				EIGHT 8					FIVE HUNDRED 500
				NINE 9					SIX HUNDRED 600
				TEN 10					SEVEN HUNDRED 700
				TWENTY 20					EIGHT HUNDRED 800
				THIRTY 30					NINE HUNDRED 900
				FORTY 40					ONE THOUSAND 1000
				FIFTY 50					TEN THOUSAND 10,000

THE 1 2 3 4 OF NUMBERS

Most people today, primitive or not, educated or not, are able to count from one to ten in their own language:

	Japanese	Hebrew	Brahui	Irish	Russian	Turkish
1	Hitotsu	Ehkhad	Asit	Oin	Odin	Bir
2	Futatsu	Shnahshah	Irat	Da	Dva	Iki
3	Mittsu	Shloshah	Musit	Tri	Tri	Uch
4	Yottsu	Arbah	Char	Kethir	Chetyrye	Dort
5	Itsutsu	Khameeshah	Panch	Koik	Pyatye	Besh
6	Muttsu	Sheeshah	Shash	Se	Shestye	Alti
7	Nanatsu	Sheevah	Haft	Secht	Semye	Yedi
8	Yattsu	Shmonah	Ocht	Hasht	Vosmye	Sekiz
9	Kokonotsu	Teeshah	Noh	Noi	Devyatye	Dokuz
10	To	Asarah	Dah	Deich	Dyesaye	On

These words from one to ten when spoken, written, or printed, regardless of the language difference—and there are countless thousands of languages—are names of amounts, or "word numbers." They indicate quantities. But they are words, not numbers. And they do not express amounts as quickly as an alphabetic letter would express a sound. An *m*, for example, would have the sound of a short hum or "em." An *s* would express a short hiss or "ess." When these alphabetic letters or sounds are combined with others they indicate a meaningful word we catch on sight; or they emit a series of sounds that communicate an idea or meaning when heard. This is the essence of written or spoken language. Moreover, word numbers when used to compute arithmetical or mathematical problems are too cumbersome to function easily.

Quantities, on the other hand, not only can be written as words, they can be expressed by symbols. The modern Arabic or European symbol for the word number *eight* is "8." The symbol for *eighty* is "80." *Eight hundred* would be "800." These symbols individually or collectively are called numerals. Individually, each represents a known quantity. Collectively—combined in various ways by addition, subtraction, multiplication, division, and other mathematical mechanisms—they constitute a systematic code for quickly determining unknown quantities, or identifying and expressing other amounts. It is much easier to compute and find the result 8000 by writing:

$$800 \div 8 \times 80 = 8000 \qquad \text{than it is to write:}$$

eight hundred divided by eight times eighty equals eight thousand.

WHEN NUMBERS BEGAN

Record keeping began long before mankind developed a writing system to communicate ideas and activities. Although people living in the Tigris-Euphrates Valley of southern Iraq marked their history with words about five thousand years ago, their predecessors, prehistoric men and women—people without a written language—kept accounts. They noted how many woolly mammoths were killed, or how many goats they herded into a cave, or how many wives, husbands, and children there were, or how many days passed between full moons. And this they did in a number of handy ways that required no particular system, sequence, or order of notation. If a man had four children, he might scratch or paint four lines on a cave wall. If he killed two woolly mammoths, he might carve two lines into the handle of his stone ax. Or if a woman herded seven goats into a cave, she might place seven rocks in a circle just to remember how many goats she had should one be missing.

THE LOOK OF NUMBERS

For tens of thousands of years, the numerical marks, scratches, and stones of primitive people slowly developed into the more ordered system of numerical notation of civilized humans. As language succeeded in becoming the chief vehicle for interpersonal communication, words, too, succeeded in becoming the chief indicator of numerical values (see chart page 7). But in the course of human development, and as people continued to further organize their activities, other means of expressing numerical amounts appeared. People used their fingers to indicate numbers from 1 through 10, and a variety of finger signs to express more complex numerical amounts or arrangements. Counting boards having grids dividing units, tens, hundreds, thousands, and so on were invented to facilitate the increased commercial use of numbers. In addition, there were abaci—counting machines in which numerical amounts were determined by the position of beads strung on a series of wires. There were systems of numerical indicators based on the positions of sticks or rope knots and other devices. Finally, symbols for numerical amounts as we know them today, and as are used throughout the world, emerged in Europe during the Middle Ages. These symbols were based on western Arabic configurations representing numbers. The western Arabic figures were derived from eastern Arabic numerals (see pages 12–15) that in turn stemmed from the numerical notations of northern India (see pages 20–23). The Indian numerals, which included the innovative *zero* sign "0," were brought westward by Arab traders during the eighth and ninth centuries A.D. Thus the Indian symbol for three thousand three hundred and thirty-three ३३३३ became the east Arabic ٣٣٣٣ which changed into western Arabic ३३३३ and finally emerged as the modern numeral *3333*.

AUTHOR'S NOTE: *Wherever scholarship was unclear making questionable a precise rendering of information, no alphabetic letter number equivalent or word number appears with a set of numerals (e.g., Brahmi pages 20–23) or with specific numerals (e.g. Egyptian hieratic pages 30–31).*

top to bottom: Modern Arabic; Sanskrit; Greek; Roman

THE NUMBERS

ARABIC

ARMENIAN

BRAHMI

CHINESE

EGYPTIAN

GOTHIC

GREEK

MAYAN

ROMAN

RUNES

SANSKRIT

THAI

TIBETAN

ARABIC

Following the death in 632 A.D. of the Prophet Mohammed, Arab horsemen swept out of their desert and attacked the world north, east, and west of them. By 732 A.D., Islam flourished from Syria to India, across North Africa, in Spain and western France. In one battle near Samarkand, just north of the present-day Russian-Afghanistan border, Arab soldiers captured Chinese papermakers whose ancestors had invented paper. The Arabs quickly learned the craft. By c. 800 A.D., Baghdad, Iraq, had become the chief source of paper west of China. Now Arab scholars began to use paper to record their knowledge and the lore of lands conquered by Arab armies.

Among these learned Arabs was mathematician Muhammad ibn al-Kwarizmi, later called Algorismus. He wrote a mathematics book which, among other things, explored the practical use of an ancient numeral system used in northern India. The book appeared in Spain during the 1100s A.D., some three hundred years after it had been written. This was about the same time that paper was becoming popular in Europe. European scholars who studied the Latin translation now viewed the Indian number system as superior to their system of Roman numerals (see pages 44–47), which had been the chief numerals of Europe since the Roman Empire. Gradually, over the next four hundred years, Arabic numerals based on the scripts of northern India which were derived from the ancient Brahmi place-value notation system (see pages 20–23), replaced everyday use of Roman numerals in Europe.

The new numerals were known as *western* Arabic or "modern European" (see page 6), the system used in most of the world today. The numerals on the following pages, derived from Brahmi, are *eastern* Arabic numbers. These numerals, too, are used today in various parts of the Middle East.

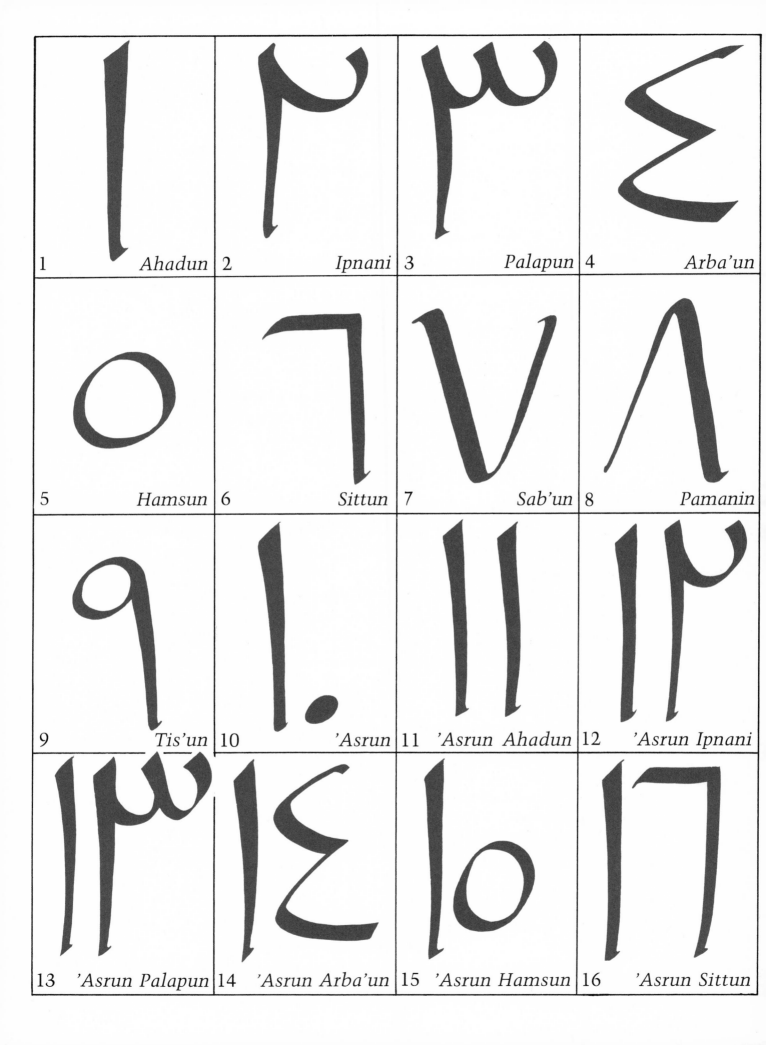

1 *Ahadun*	2 *Ipnani*	3 *Palapun*	4 *Arba'un*
5 *Hamsun*	6 *Sittun*	7 *Sab'un*	8 *Pamanin*
9 *Tis'un*	10 *'Asrun*	11 *'Asrun Ahadun*	12 *'Asrun Ipnani*
13 *'Asrun Palapun*	14 *'Asrun Arba'un*	15 *'Asrun Hamsun*	16 *'Asrun Sittun*

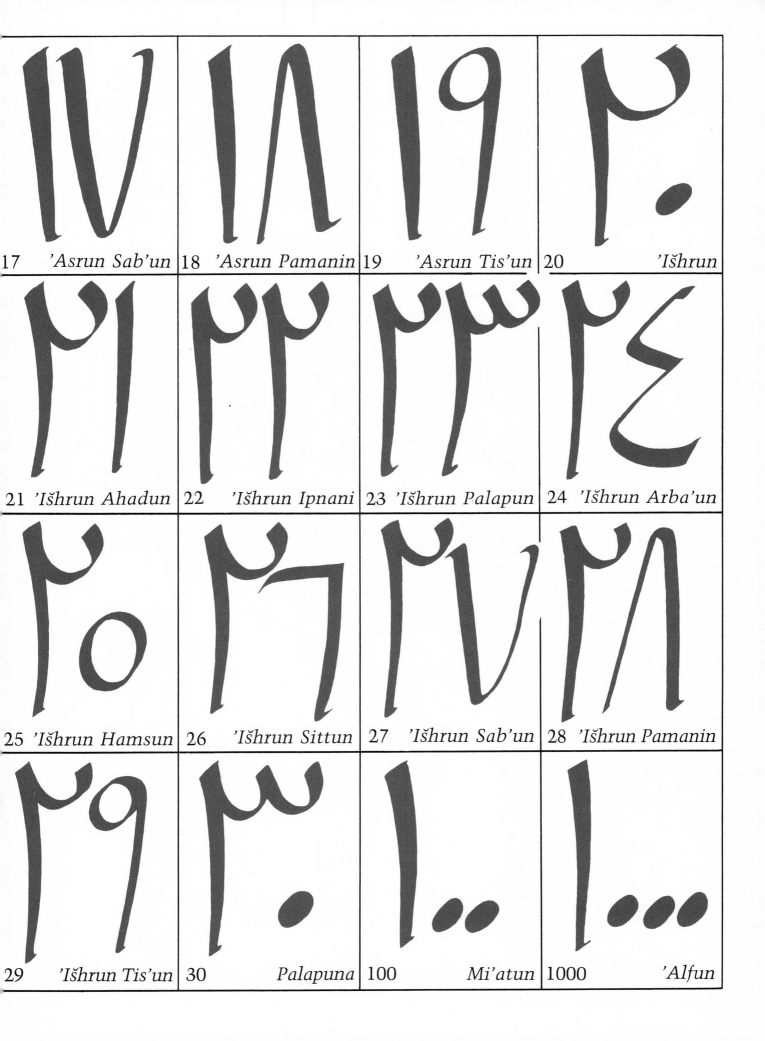

17 'Asrun Sab'un	18 'Asrun Pamanin	19 'Asrun Tis'un	20 'Išhrun
21 'Išhrun Ahadun	22 'Išhrun Ipnani	23 'Išhrun Palapun	24 'Išhrun Arba'un
25 'Išhrun Hamsun	26 'Išhrun Sittun	27 'Išhrun Sab'un	28 'Išhrun Pamanin
29 'Išhrun Tis'un	30 Palapuna	100 Mi'atun	1000 'Alfun

ARMENIAN

Armenia is a land as ancient as the stories of the Old Testament patriarchs. Here, in a rugged area spanning the Turkish-Russian frontier between the Black and Caspian seas, north of Iraq and west of Iran, is Mount Ararat where biblical Noah came to rest after the great flood. And here, Haik, a descendant of Noah, is said to have founded the first Armenian kingdom.

For two thousand years, beginning in the 800s B.C., unsubdued Armenians were tormented by Assyrian, Persian, Greek, Roman, Mongol, Arab, Turk, and Russian invaders. Their final indignity came in April 1915 when Muslim Ottoman Turks, embroiled in World War I, decided to obliterate their difficult Christian Armenian subjects, accusing them of helping the Russian enemy. Armenian men were murdered in every town and village. Much of the remaining population—old and sick people, women and children—were force-marched into the Iranian desert where thousands died. Those who survived and did not flee to America and elsewhere were absorbed into the Russian and Turkish realms.

Armenian identity remains strong, nourished by oppression, close church ties—Armenians were converted to Christianity by Saint Gregory the Illuminator, c. 300 A.D.—and a distinctive language and alphabet. One hundred years following conversion, Mesrop Mashtots, a monk, devised an alphabet and translated the Bible into Armenian. Thereafter, the Armenian Church began to encourage further literary adventures which helped to create a large body of Armenian religious literature. In this context, each alphabet letter was assigned a number value. The letter-numbers were used to identify biblical passages, psalms, chapters, paragraphs, and the like, but not for calculation or abstract mathematics.

(A) 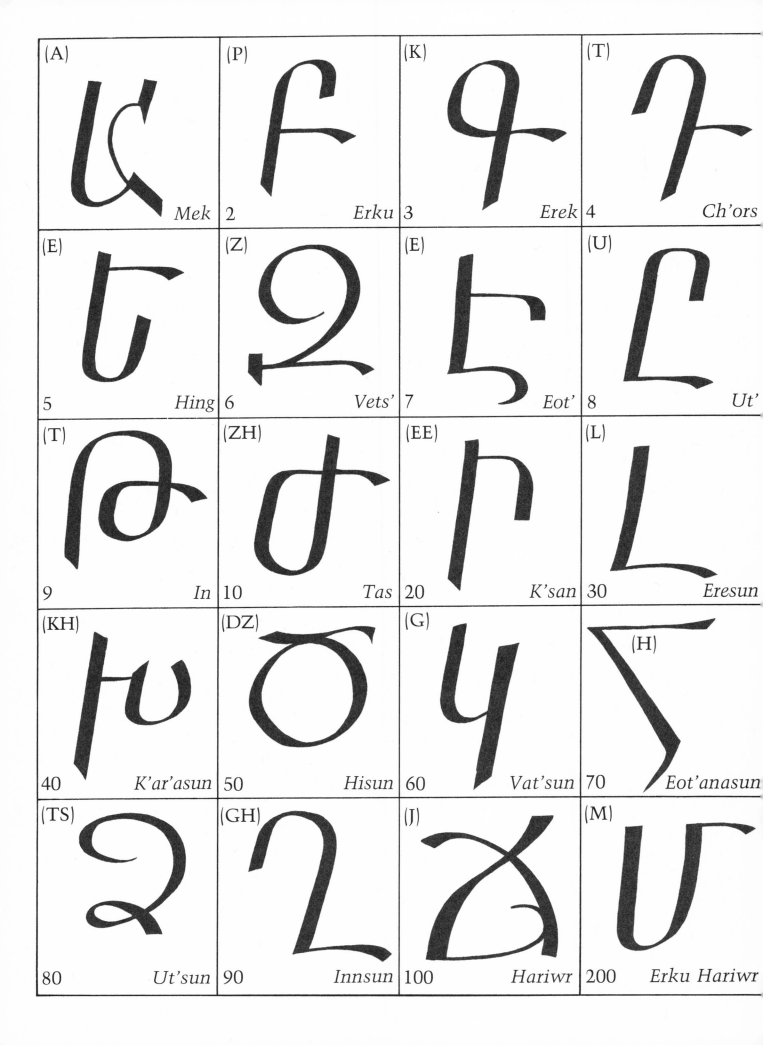 *Mek*	(P) 2 *Erku*	(K) 3 *Erek*	(T) 4 *Ch'ors*
(E) 5 *Hing*	(Z) 6 *Vets'*	(E) 7 *Eot'*	(U) 8 *Ut'*
(T) 9 *In*	(ZH) 10 *Tas*	(EE) 20 *K'san*	(L) 30 *Eresun*
(KH) 40 *K'ar'asun*	(DZ) 50 *Hisun*	(G) 60 *Vat'sun*	(H) 70 *Eot'anasun*
(TS) 80 *Ut'sun*	(GH) 90 *Innsun*	(J) 100 *Hariwr*	(M) 200 *Erku Hariwr*

(H) 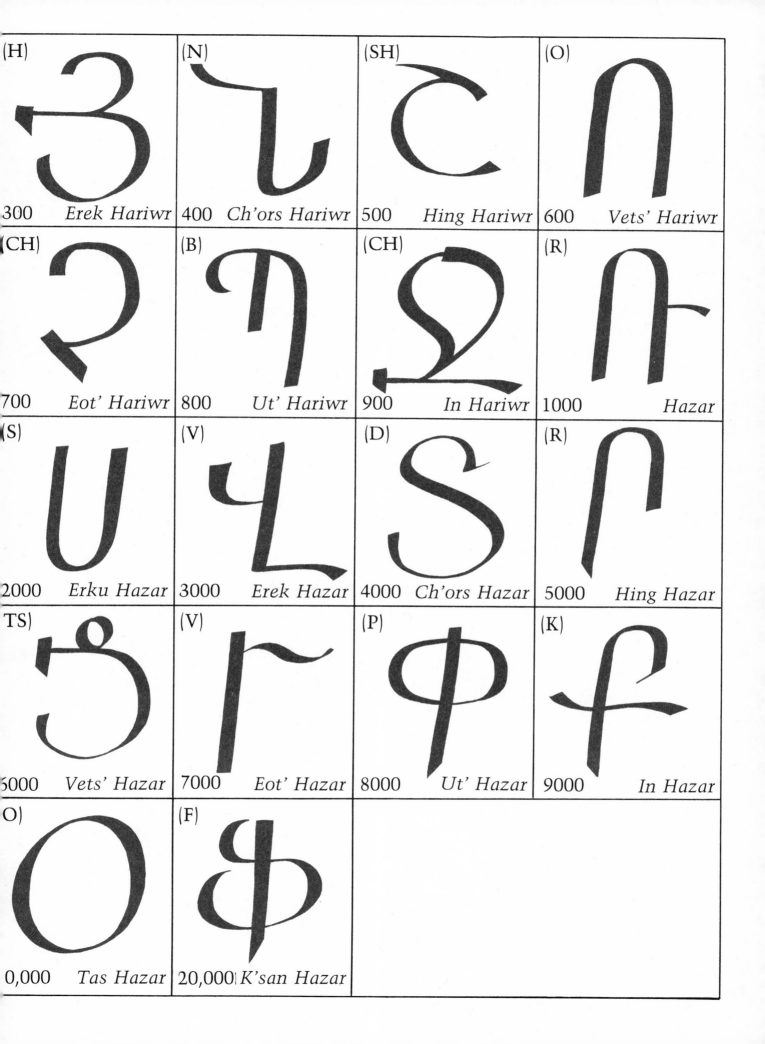	(N)	(SH)	(O)
300　　Erek Hariwr	400　　Ch'ors Hariwr	500　　Hing Hariwr	600　　Vets' Hariwr
(CH)	(B)	(CH)	(R)
700　　Eot' Hariwr	800　　Ut' Hariwr	900　　In Hariwr	1000　　Hazar
(S)	(V)	(D)	(R)
2000　　Erku Hazar	3000　　Erek Hazar	4000　　Ch'ors Hazar	5000　　Hing Hazar
(TS)	(V)	(P)	(K)
6000　　Vets' Hazar	7000　　Eot' Hazar	8000　　Ut' Hazar	9000　　In Hazar
(O)	(F)		
10,000　　Tas Hazar	20,000　　K'san Hazar		

BRAHMI

During the reign of King Asoka (c. 255–235 B.C.), who ruled over most of India, Buddhism became the official Indian religion, and Brahmi, a written form of spoken Sanskrit (see pages 52–55), became the dominant Indian script. Buddhism, founded to oppose the powerful Brahmins, the upper strata of Indian society, would one day be replaced by Hinduism; Sanskrit would cease to be the spoken language; but Brahmi, the writing of the educated aristocracy, would seed the many various Indian alphabets, become the origin of our modern-world Arabic numerals, and provide the basic system for notating numerical amounts (see page 6).

Brahmi and Kharosthi were the two written forms of Sanskrit in ancient India that contained numerals. The Kharosthi script, read from right to left, flourished for about six hundred years (400 B.C.–200 A.D.) as a written language used in business transactions. It was unrelated to our modern numerals.

Brahmi, on the other hand, read from left to right, was the earliest known alphabet to use single symbols indicating numerical amounts. Eventually, a zero would be added to the Brahmi number alphabet and all number symbols except 0 through 9 would be eliminated. Every possible combination of numbers and their amounts would be expressed with these ten symbols in a place-value notation system. The system was simple. Each numerical value—thousands, hundreds, tens, units, and so on—had a place. From left to right: Fourth place was reserved for thousands, third place for hundreds, second place for tens, and first place for units. Thus, the number one thousand six hundred twenty-four—1624—was written long ago in Brahmi ７６２Ƴ , much as it is written today. And although the actual Brahmi numerical symbols are no longer in common use, the ancient Brahmi system for expressing numerical amounts is used throughout the modern world.

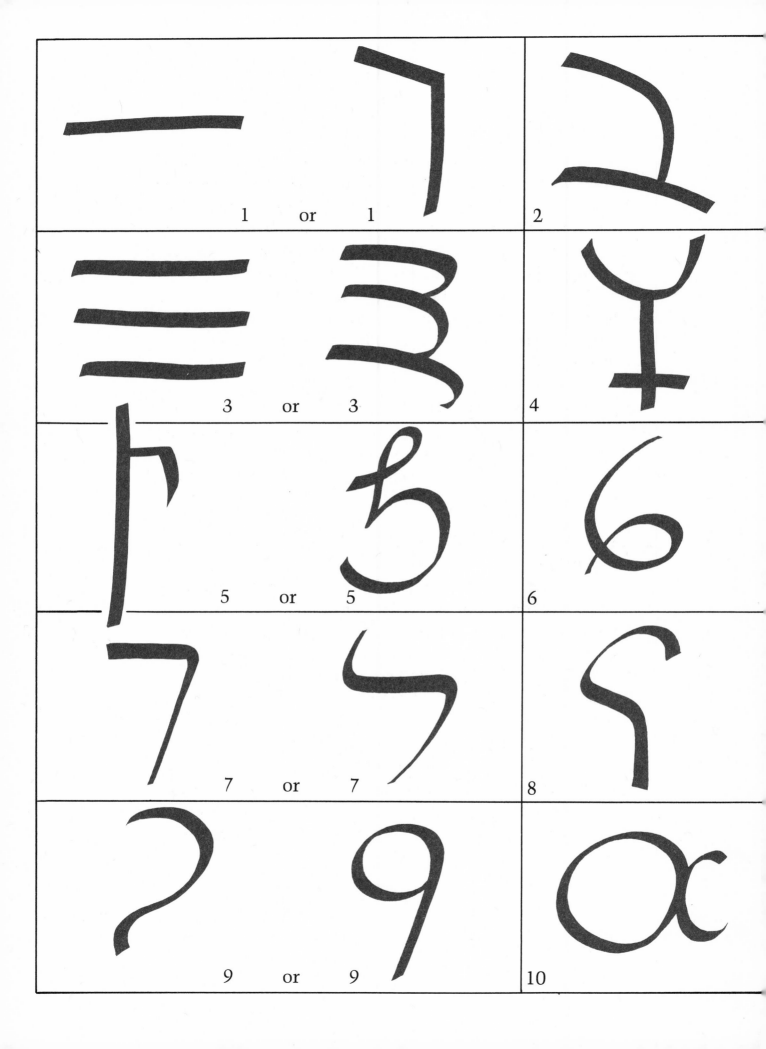

1   or   1   2

3   or   3   4

5   or   5   6

7   or   7   8

9   or   9   10

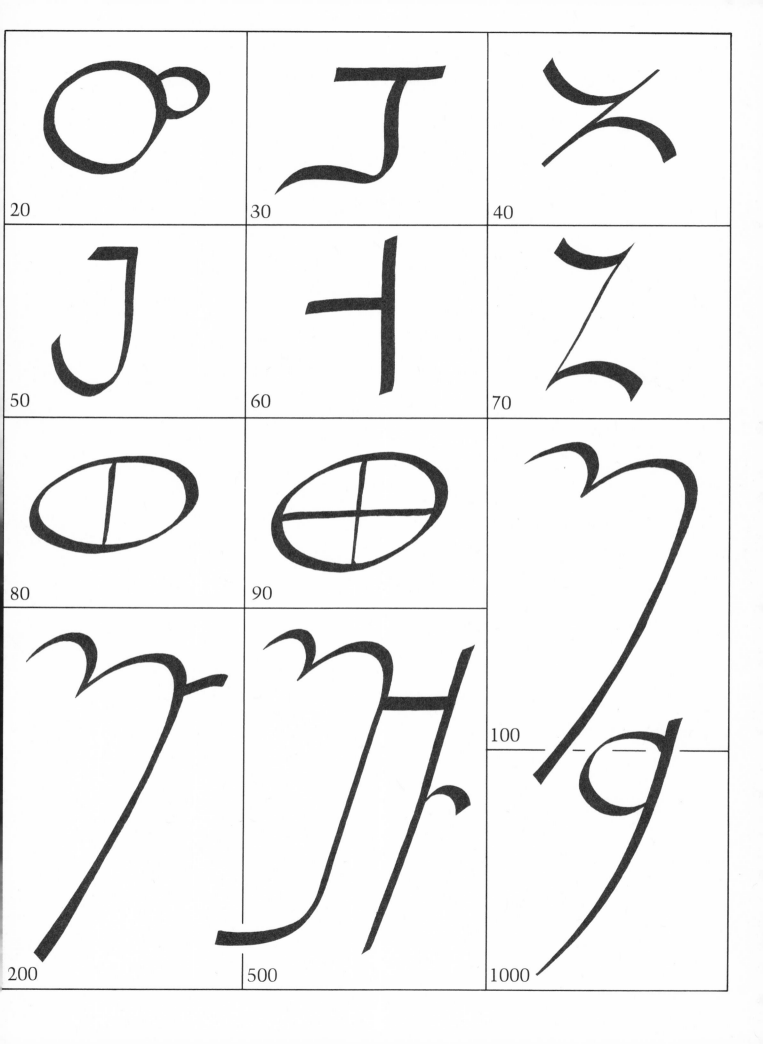

CHINESE

Chinese writing was about three thousand years old—almost beyond measure—when in c. 500 B.C. Chinese numerals emerged. Buddha and Confucius were then living out their lives in Asia. Their ideas and actions would impact upon the entire Oriental world and beyond. Until Buddhist influence flowed from India into China and other parts of Asia between c. 100–500 A.D., Chinese numerals dominated much of the Asian world. After widespread acceptance of Buddha as God, the use of Chinese numerals by non-Chinese ethnic groups vanished. Even the Chinese themselves absorbed some Indian numeral characterization. Only the Japanese retained Chinese numerals in their own written language. In any event, Chinese numeration developed into four categories, each having different functions, all of which could be, and often were, used simultaneously:

Stick numerals, a simple form of notation no longer used, evolved from a widespread custom of grouping wood sticks on a grid-marked counting board. The zero digit seen on page 27 first appeared during the 1200s A.D. after more than a thousand years of *stick* computations.

Basic numerals, an ordinary writing form in which the number and the word for the number are represented by the same written sign. These are the most commonly used Chinese numerals.

Official numerals, very decorative characters used for important contracts, currency, deeds, and the like, to lend importance to the documents and prevent fraud or counterfeiting.

Commercial numerals, used chiefly by business people to make informal notations of prices, product weights, profits, losses; send bills; or record other day-to-day commercial transactions.

Beyond these numeration categories, the present-day People's Republic of China is continuing its effort to simplify written Chinese while introducing the standard, worldwide practice of using Arabic numerals.

I. BASIC NUMERALS
HSIAO-HSIEH
(ordinary writing)

		五 5　　Wu	八 8　　Pa	百 100　Pai
一 1　　I	三 3　　San	六 6　　Liu	九 9　　Chiu	千 1000　Ch'ien
二 2　　Erh	四 4　　Szu	七 7　　Ch'i	十 10　　Shih	萬万 10,000　Wan

II. OFFICIAL NUMERALS
TA-HSIEH
(seal writing)

		伍 5　　Wu	捌 8　　Pa	百 100　Pai
壹 1　　I	參 3　　San	陸 6　　Liu	玖 9　　Chiu	仟 1000　Ch'ien
貳 2　　Erh	肆 4　　Szu	柒 7　　Ch'i	拾 10　　Shih	萬 10,000　Wan

III. COMMERCIAL NUMERALS
SU-CHOU MA-TZU
(Suchow weight numbers)

0 *Ling*	5 *Wu*	8 *Pa*	100 *Pai*
1 *I*	3 *San*	6 *Liu*	9 *Chiu*	1000 *Ch'ien*
2 *Erh*	4 *Szu*	7 *Ch'i*	10 *Shih*	10,000 *Wan*

IV. STICK NUMERALS

0 *Ling*	5 *Wu*	8 *Pa*	100 *Pai*
1 *I*	3 *San*	6 *Liu*	9 *Chiu*	1000 *Ch'ien*
2 *Erh*	4 *Szu*	7 *Ch'i*	10 *Shih*	10,000 *Wan*

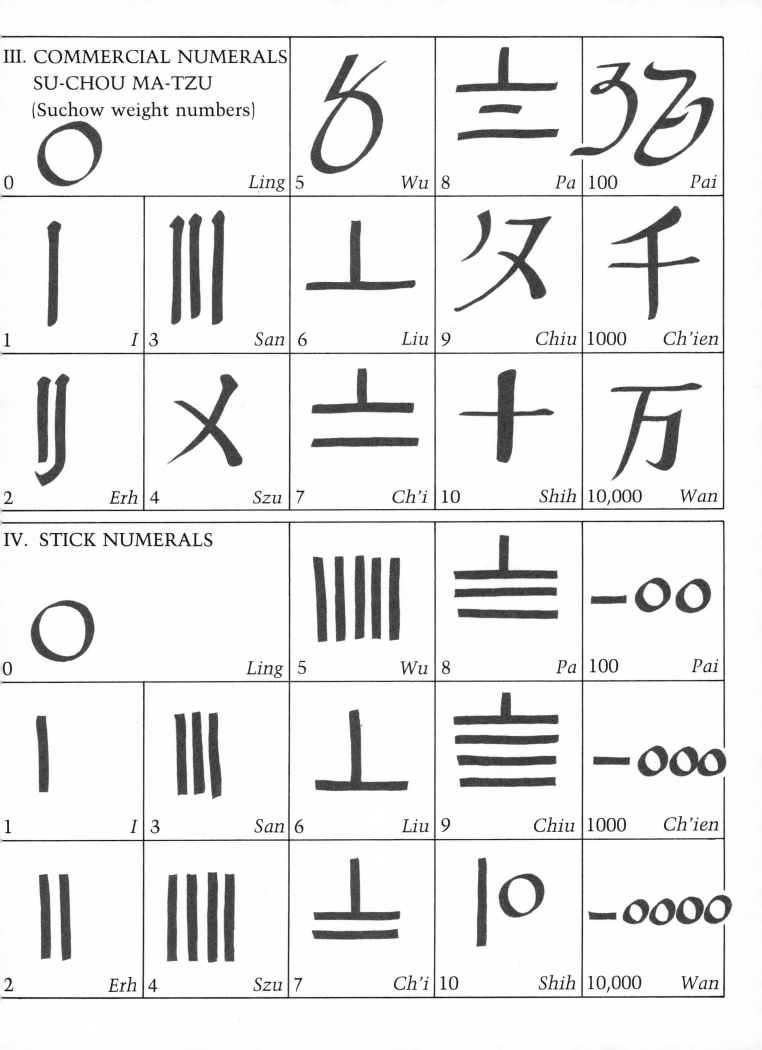

EGYPTIAN

From the earliest flicker of Egyptian civilization through the Old Kingdom period at Memphis (5000–2200 B.C.), a span of 2800 years, priests developed, perfected, and finally discarded hieroglyphic or picture writing to express themselves. Common people hardly ever read or wrote hieroglyphics.

Numerical amounts written in hieroglyphics were somewhat more cumbersome than *ideograms*, in which, for example, the symbol of a mouth was used to represent *mouth*; or *phonograms*, in which the symbol of a mouth was used to represent the sound *re* because the word *mouth* in ancient Egypt began with an *r*; but simpler than *determinatives* in which the hieroglyph for *mouth* was used to clarify the meaning of a string of hieroglyphs having several meanings. Numbers had a specific set of symbols (see page 6) and a specific sequence to indicate a numerical amount. Using hieroglyphic numerical-unit symbols, the number 3333—read from left to right—was written:

Between 2200 and 1000 B.C., during the Middle Kingdom-New Empire periods, the priests developed a rhythmical shorthand or cursive script to replace the old hieroglyphs. It was called hieratic—or the "writing of the priests." Demotic writing, "writing of the people," would not emerge until the Ptolemaic or Greek period in Egyptian history (332–30 B.C.). The hieratic numerals seen on the following pages form a "ciphered" system. Numbers from 1 to 10 each have a symbol as do numbers 10–90, 100–900, 1000–9000, and so on. Using hieratic numerical-unit symbols or ciphers, the number 3333—read from left to right—was written:

Hieratic writing was simpler than hieroglyphic writing. And the writing of numerical amounts in hieratic was simpler, too. Still, it was not as precise as the Brahmi place-value notation that would one day sweep the western world in the Arabic numeral system.

Modern Egyptians speak and write Arabic. Their number symbols are no longer hieratic but the familiar western Arabic numerals.

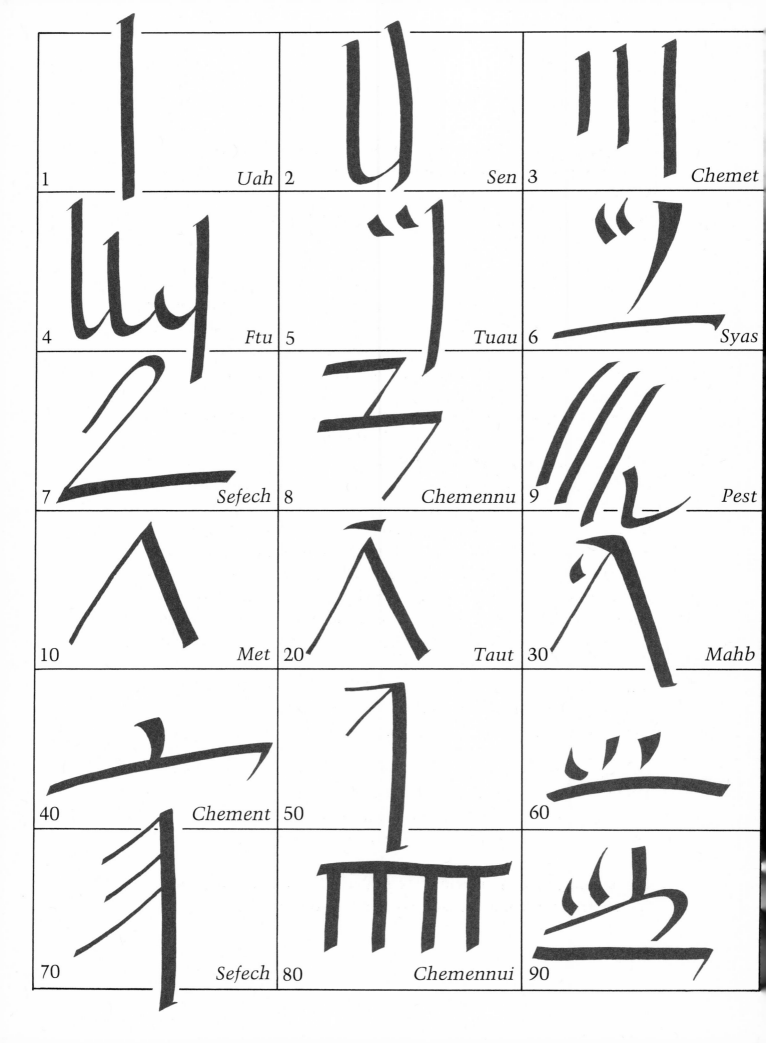

1	Uah	2	Sen	3	Chemet
4	Ftu	5	Tuau	6	Syas
7	Sefech	8	Chemennu	9	Pest
10	Met	20	Taut	30	Mahb
40	Chement	50		60	
70	Sefech	80	Chemennui	90	

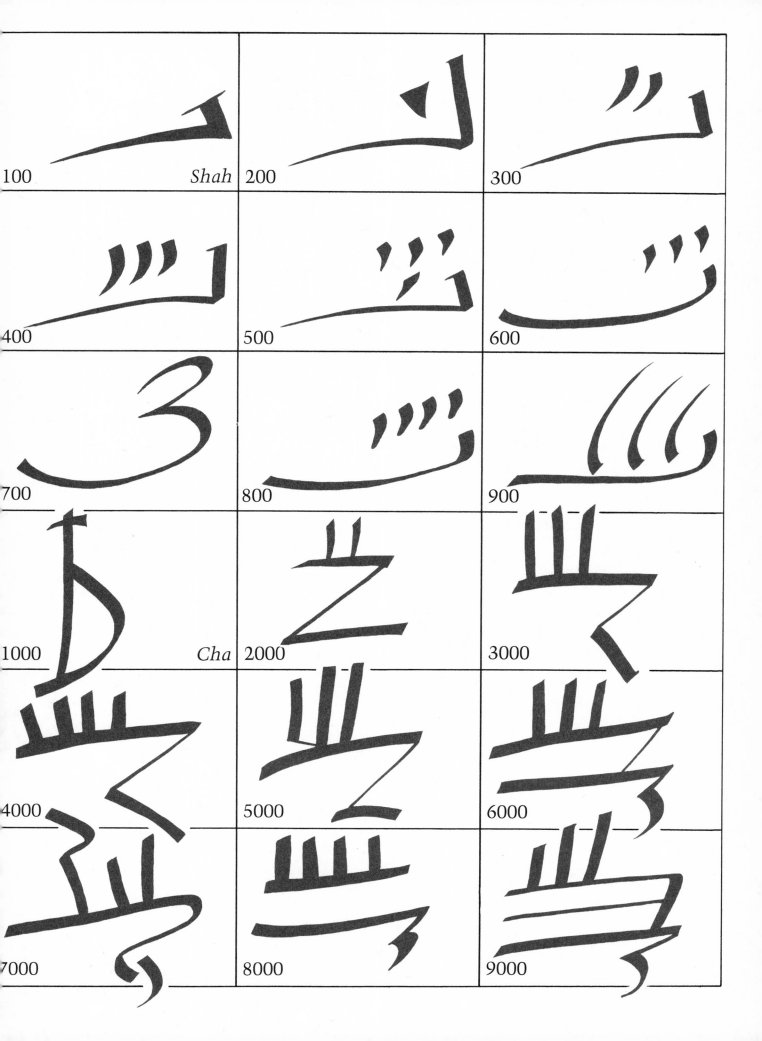

100 *Shah*	200	300
400	500	600
700	800	900
1000 *Cha*	2000	3000
4000	5000	6000
7000	8000	9000

GOTHIC

The Goths were an aggressive collection of Germanic tribes who moved from the Baltic Sea area during the 200s A.D. to just north of the Black Sea. There they collided with Greek culture and the onrush of Christianity. About a hundred years later they split into two groups: west, or Visigoths, and east, or Ostrogoths.

Driven westward by the Huns, the Visigoths, led by Alaric I, invaded Italy, sacking Rome in 410. Eventually, they reached Spain where they ended their often violent migration. By the 700s, they had disappeared, becoming part of the Iberian ethnic mix. The Ostrogoths, overrun by the Huns, resettled in present-day Hungary. Theodoric, an Ostrogothic king, conquered Italy in 493 and made Ravenna his capital. The Ostrogoths were driven from Italy about sixty years later and also disappeared, melting into the ethnic composition of Hungary.

The strong Christian strain of the Goths was the work of Bishop Ulfilas, a fourth-century convert to Christianity. Visigoth Ulfilas brought his learning and Christian devotion to the pagan Goths. Having converted much of their multitude, he then translated the Bible for their use. To make the Germanic Gothic language Bible more readily understood, he invented an alphabet consisting of Greek, Latin, and runic letters. These same letters when capped by a dash or bracketed with dots became numbers. But they were not numbers for performing arithmetical functions or keeping accounts. Roman numerals served those purposes. Gothic letter-numbers were used to identify biblical chapters in much the same way the Armenians used letter-numbers (see pages 16–19).

(A)	(B)	(G)
Ā	Ƀ	Γ̄
1 *Ains*	2 *Twa*	3 *Preis*
(D)	(E)	(Q)
đ	Ē	Ū
4 *Fidwor*	5 *Fimf*	6 *Saihs*
(Z)	(H)	(PS)
Z̄	ħ	Ψ̄
7 *Sibun*	8 *Ahtau*	9 *Niun*
(I)	(K)	(L)
Ī	K̄	Λ̄
10 *Taihun*	20 *Twai-Tigjus*	30 *Preo-Tigjus*
(M)	(N)	(J)
M̄	N̄	Ḡ
40 *Fidwor-Tigjus*	50 *Fimf-Tigjus*	60 *Saihs-Tigjus*

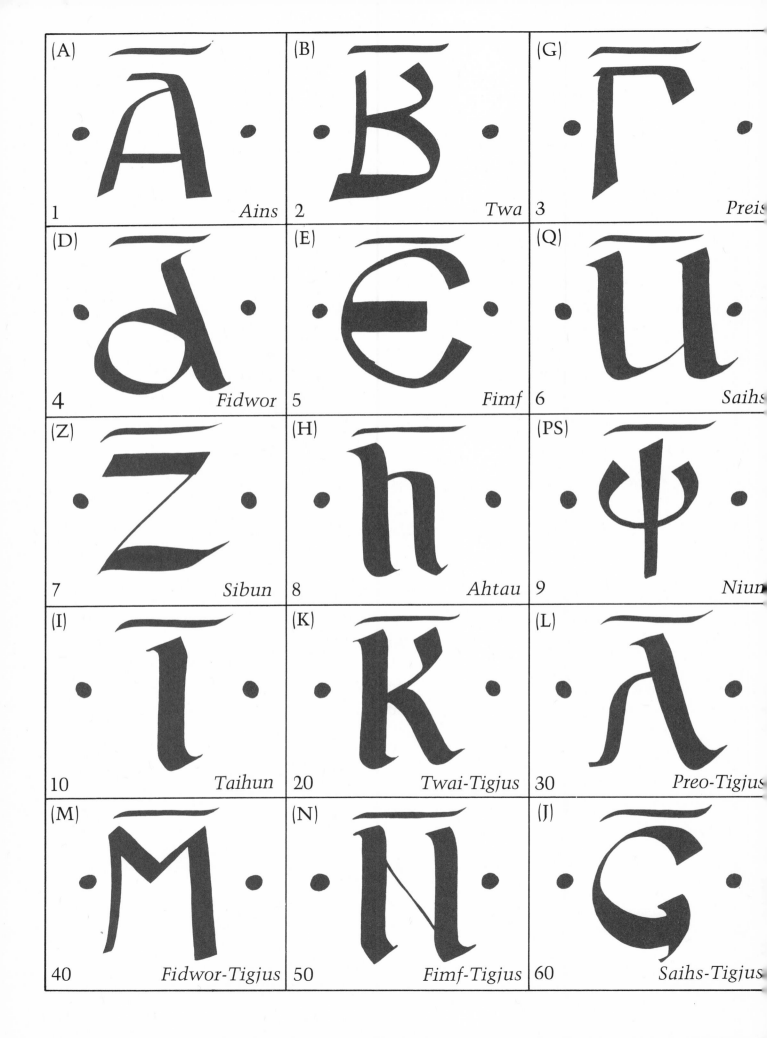

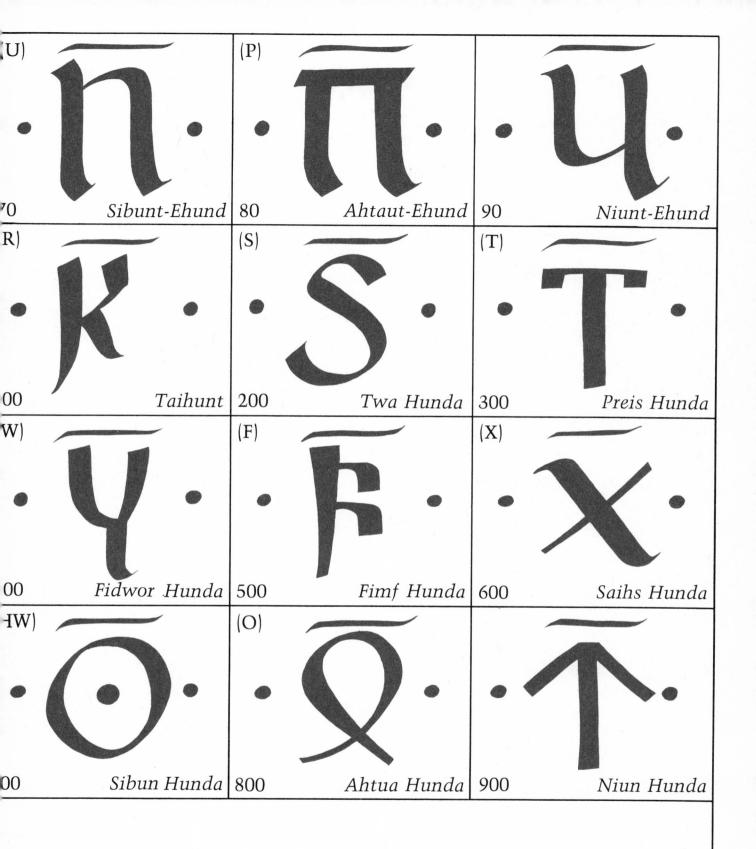

(U)	(P)	
70 Sibunt-Ehund	80 Ahtaut-Ehund	90 Niunt-Ehund
(R)	(S)	(T)
00 Taihunt	200 Twa Hunda	300 Preis Hunda
(W)	(F)	(X)
00 Fidwor Hunda	500 Fimf Hunda	600 Saihs Hunda
(HW)	(O)	
00 Sibun Hunda	800 Ahtua Hunda	900 Niun Hunda

GREEK

The ancient Greeks were the first to use alphabetic letters as numbers. Unlike older civilizations (e.g., India, China, Egypt) who used numbers to work out everyday problems, the Greeks used their numbers to explore abstract ideas that had no practical application. They relied on a counting board or *abakion*—an abacus—to solve their practical problems. The Greeks became the first to enter the realm of pure mathematics. And this they did before the Roman Republic was founded in 509 B.C.

Some time during the 600s B.C., Thales, a Greek thinker, promoted the idea that a relationship existed between natural things and the space they occupied. He set about to prove the truth of his notion by careful reasoning or logic. Thales' logic led him to analyze triangles to prove that solutions arrived at by simple, practical, age-old geometrical formulae were "truths." Eventually, the Greeks became so preoccupied with philosophy, logic, and pure mathematics that these became basic to their education. Underlying this direction of Greek intellect was their basic concept that goodness, beauty, and truth were inseparable; and that the human race, the center of the universe, the measure of all things, was the embodiment of goodness, truth, and beauty. Pursuing these beliefs, Pythagoras examined the nature of numbers during the 500s B.C. He proved that the square of the hypotenuse of a right triangle was equal to the sum of its sides. Two hundred years later, Euclid defined geometry as an exact discipline, while Archimedes unlocked mysteries of integral calculus, among other things. Later, Ptolemy and Diophantos gave the world trigonometry and algebra. Greek philosopher-mathematicians such as these laid the foundation for modern higher mathematics. And today's mathematicians explore the unknown using Greek alphabetic numerals.

UNITS ▶	$\bar{\alpha}$ (alpha) 1 *Heîs, Mía,* or *Hén*	$\bar{\beta}$ (beta) 2 *Dýo*	$\bar{\gamma}$ (gamma) 3 *Treîs* or *Tria*
$\bar{\delta}$ (delta) 4 *Téttares* or *Tettara*	$\bar{\epsilon}$ (epsilon) 5 *Pénte*	$\bar{\varsigma}$ (vau) 6 *Héx*	$\bar{\zeta}$ (zeta) 7 *Heptá*
$\bar{\eta}$ (eta) 8 *Oktố*	$\bar{\vartheta}$ (theta) 9 *Ennéa*	TENS ▶	$\bar{\iota}$ (iota) 10 *Deka*
$\bar{\kappa}$ (kappa) 20 *Eíkosi*	$\bar{\lambda}$ (lambda) 30 *Triákonta*	$\bar{\mu}$ (mu) 40 *Tettarakonta*	$\bar{\nu}$ (nu) 50 *Pentếkonta*
$\bar{\xi}$ (xi) 60 *Hexếkonta*	$\bar{o}$ (omicron) 70 *Hebdomếkonta*	$\bar{\pi}$ (pi) 80 *Ogdoékonta*	$\bar{\varsigma}$ (koppa) 90 *Emenékonta*

HUNDREDS ▶	$\bar{\rho}$ (rho) 100 Hekatón	$\bar{\sigma}$ (sigma) 200 Diakósioi	$\bar{\tau}$ (tau) 300 Triakósioi
$\bar{\upsilon}$ (upsilon) 400 Tetrakósioi	$\bar{\varphi}$ (phi) 500 Pentakósioi	$\bar{\chi}$ (chi) 600 Hexakósioi	$\bar{\psi}$ (psi) 700 Heptakósioi
$\bar{\omega}$ (omega) 800 Oktakósioi	$\bar{\lambda}$ (sampi) 900 Enneakósioi	THOUSANDS ▶	α 1000 Chílioi
β 2000 Dischílioi	γ 3000 Trischílioi	TENS OF THOUSANDS ▶	$\ddot{\alpha}$ 10,000 Mýrioi
$\ddot{\beta}$ 20,000 Eikosimýrioi	$\ddot{\gamma}$ 30,000 Triakontamýrioi	FRACTIONS ▶	$\iota'\ \frac{1}{10}$ $\kappa'\ \frac{1}{20}$ $\lambda'\ \frac{1}{30}$ $\mu'\ \frac{1}{40}$ $\nu'\ \frac{1}{50}$ $\xi'\ \frac{1}{60}$ $o'\ \frac{1}{70}$ $\pi'\ \frac{1}{80}$ $\mathcal{G}'\ \frac{1}{90}$

MAYA

Between the Age of Alexander the Great and the Roman legalization of Christianity (356 B.C.–311 A.D.) the Maya Indians of Central America mastered reading, writing, and arithmetic. They were the first people in the Western Hemisphere to grasp the mysteries and possibilities of pure knowledge.

The Maya had spent about two thousand years developing their intellectual powers. By 300 B.C., Maya priests not only had achieved hieroglyphic writing, made profound astronomical observations, formed a distinct style of stone architecture, and built cities, but also had invented two calendars of startling precision. Using their astronomical-arithmetical know-how, the Maya designed a regular 365-day year calendar having approximately 30-day months; and a 260-day sacred calendar having 20-day months. Both calendars included allowances for minute corrections dealing with the accurate recording of time.

The strength of the extraordinary Mayan intellect lay in a thorough understanding of mathematics, which they perfected to compute time accurately, chiefly for religious purposes. In some instances their knowledge seemed to exceed more advanced European and Asiatic civilizations of which they were apparently ignorant. Mayan use of a symbol to signify no amount, nothing, "zero," was as indigenous to them as elephants are to India. Throughout their history, which faded before the Spanish conquests of the 1500s, the Maya used a *vigesimal* arithmetical system—a system with a twenty-numeral base, 0 to 19—instead of, for example, a *decimal* system with a base of 10 numerals, 0 to 9. And this they expressed in one of two ways: the dot/bar system (see page 42) for calculation, and the head-variant system (see page 43) to symbolize a quantity. The dot/bar system could be compared to the Roman system of notation (see pages 44–47). The head-variant symbols could be likened to our modern-day use of Arabic numerals.

DOT/BAR SYSTEM

0	1 *Hun*	2 *Ca*	3 *Ox*
4 *Can*	5 *Ho*	6 *Uac*	7 *Uuc*
8 *Uaxac*	9 *Bolon*	10 *Lahun*	11 *Buluc*
12 *Lah-ca*	13 *Ox-lahun*	14 *Can-lahun*	15 *Ho-lahun*
16 *Uac-lahun*	17 *Uuc-lahun*	18 *Uaxac-lahun*	19 *Bolon-lahun*

ROMAN

Legend says that Romulus and Remus, twin boys brought up by a she-wolf, founded Rome in 753 B.C. The area was farmed at the time by Latini, not Romani or Romans. However puzzling these origins seem to be, it is known that Romans established a republic in 509 B.C. For the next eight hundred to nine hundred years, Rome and Romans forged one of the most vigorous empires in world history. Broad sections of Europe, Britain, North Africa, the Middle East, and Asia Minor fell under Roman dominion. Roman law, engineering, and political organization became foundation blocks of modern society. And although the ancient Romans did not survive into modern times, some of their innovations did, including their numerical notation system. Roman numerals are used today to number picture plates in books, to identify founding dates on college seals and building cornerstones, to indicate the hour on sundials and clocks, or the year of the copyrighting of a film, and for other, chiefly decorative purposes.

Roman numbers were simple to construct but clumsy to compute with and notate. Adding and subtracting were easy. Multiplying and dividing were difficult. Seven alphabetic letters used in combination formed all amounts except 100 million or infinity: I (1), V (5), X (10), L (50), C (100), D (500), M (1000). Low numbers followed high numbers for addition: VI = 5 + 1 = 6. High numbers followed low numbers for subtraction: IV = 1 − 5 = 4. Multiples of 1000 were indicated by a *vinculum* or top bar: $\overline{\text{DCCLVIII}}$CMXXIV = 758,924. Until the end of the Renaissance in Europe, c. 1500s, Roman numerals were the most commonly used numerical symbols in the western world. After the 1500s, Arabic numerals, based on the Brahmi symbol or "cipher" place-value system (see page 21), became the chief number "language" of the western world.

1 *Unus/Una/Unum*	2 *Duo/Duae/Duo*	3 *Tres/Tria*	4 *Quattuor*
5 *Quinque*	6 *Sex*	7 *Septem*	8 *Octo*
9 *Novem*	10 *Decem*	11 *Undecim*	12 *Duodecim*
13 *Tredecim*	14 *Quattuordecim*	15 *Quindecim*	16 *Sedecim*
17 *Septendecim*	18 *Octodecim* or *Duodeviginti*	19 *Novendecim* or *Undeviginti*	20 *Viginti*

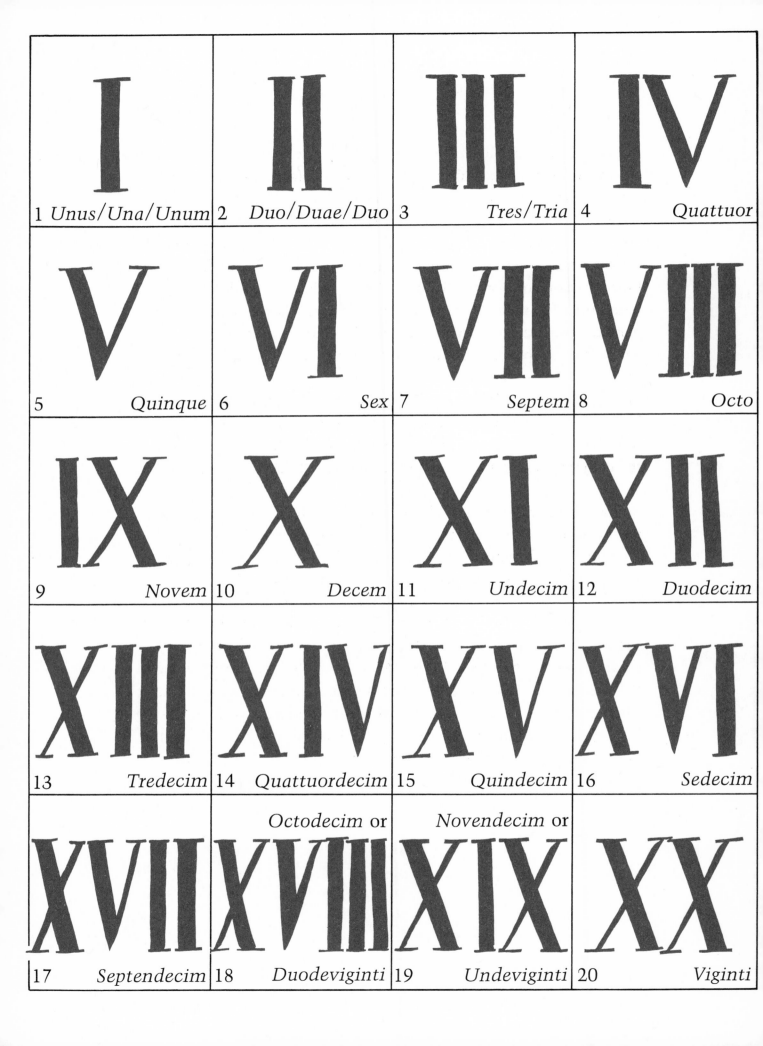

XXX	**XL**	**L**	**LX**
30 *Triginta*	40 *Quadraginta*	50 *Quinquaginta*	60 *Sexaginta*
LXX	**LXXX**	**XC**	**C**
70 *Septuaginta*	80 *Octoginta*	90 *Nonaginta*	100 *Centum*
Ducenti/Ducentae/ **CC**	**CCC**	**CD**	**D**
200 *Ducenta*	300 *Trecenti*	400 *Quadringenti*	500 *Quingenti*
DC	**DCC**	**DCCC**	**CM**
600 *Sescenti*	700 *Septingenti*	800 *Octingenti*	900 *Nongenti*
M	(vinculum) **X̄**	(vinculum) **C̄**	**∞**
1000 *Mille*	10,000 *Decem Millia*	100,000 *Centum Millia*	100 *Million* or *Infinity*

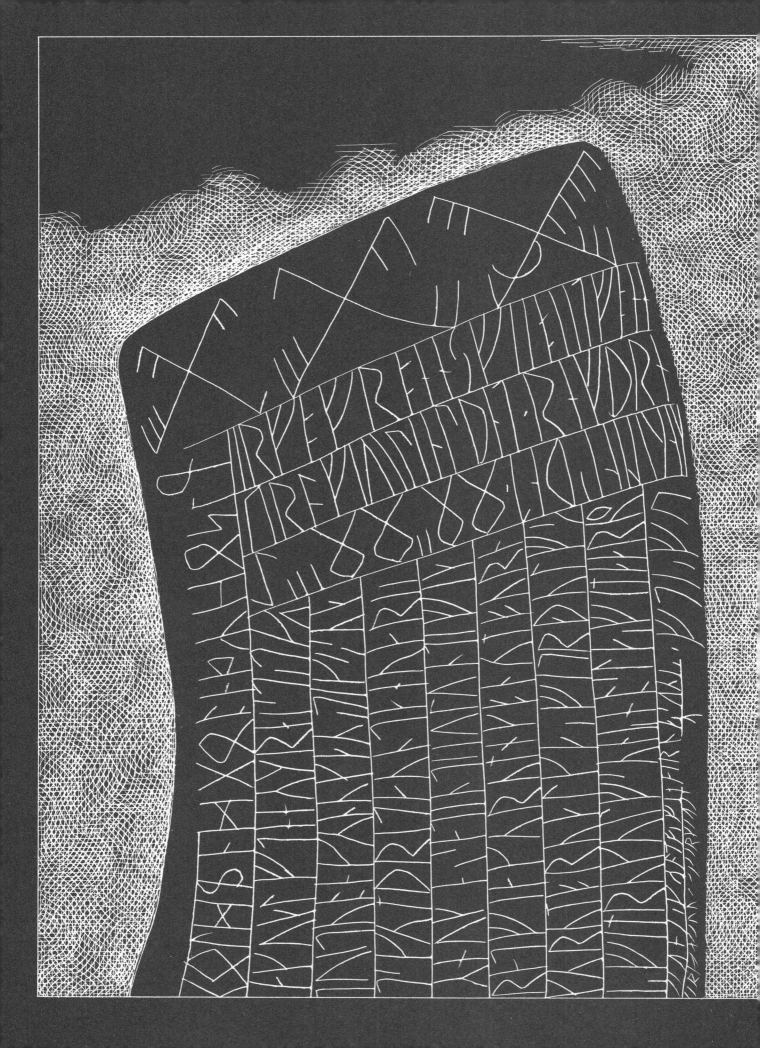

RUNES

Few scholars are willing to make precise judgments as to why or when runic numbers—and the runic alphabet itself—appeared. Nor are they clear as to the exact use and meaning of runes. Runic alphabetic characters, which are interchangeable with numerals, emerged in northern Europe among German tribes in c. 200–300 A.D., roughly during the period in which the declining Roman Empire had split into two parts, East and West.

The style of runes, which seems to relate to Latin alphabets of northern Italy, flourished for some 1200 years among peoples who had not yet accepted the doctrine of a Supreme Being or One God. In Germany, France, Spain, England, Denmark, Norway, and Sweden, where runes were most prevalent, those who used runic writing were considered heathens who practiced strange and mysterious ceremonies. Included in these so-called pagan rites were codelike, secret inscriptions—numbers and letters—carved into wood or scratched on stone. Indeed, the word *rune*, or *run* in old Germanic and Scandinavian dialects, meant "secret."

During the nearly eight-hundred-year span of the Middle Ages (c. 500–1300 A.D.), runic writing practically disappeared in Europe but persisted in Scandinavia for at least another one hundred years. Runic numbers seem to have had little to do with the amounts or costs of things. In fact, they had no apparent numerical value. Instead, they apparently had no other use than fortune-telling and perhaps dating historical events, not to mention the casting of magic spells. Although runes did occasionally appear on coins and manuscripts, they are chiefly identified with pagan worship thriving in the midst of Judeo-Christian societies.

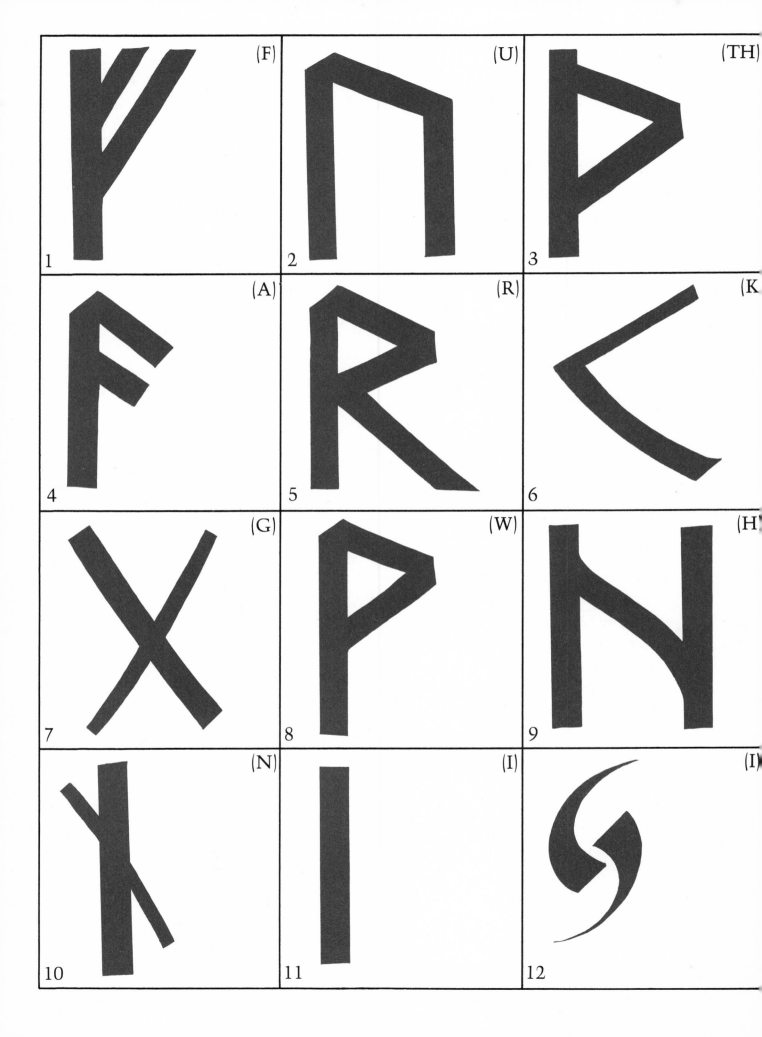

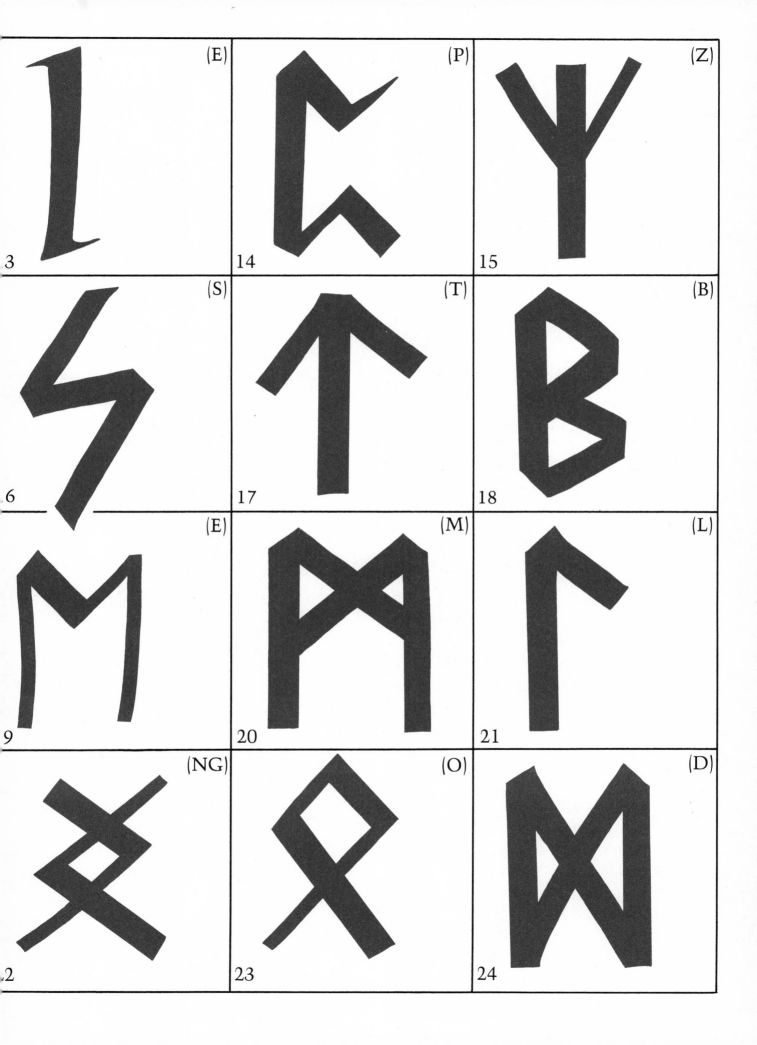

(E)	(P)	(Z)
3	14	15

(S)	(T)	(B)
6	17	18

(E)	(M)	(L)
9	20	21

(NG)	(O)	(D)
2	23	24

SANSKRIT

About 3500 years ago (c. 1500 B.C.), restless Aryans left their home at the edge of the Caspian Sea in present-day Iran. One group headed west toward Europe. The other group moved eastward toward India, invading the vast subcontinent and conquering the people who farmed the fertile banks of the Ganges River. The priests and warriors among them were the ruling groups. Eventually, they became the highest caste of Indian society. Known as Brahmins, they imposed on the region their own language, Sanskrit, written in their own script, Brahmi. Sanskrit was a tongue with roots deep in the dim past of Aryan history.

To protect their rule, the powerful Brahmins promoted the ignorance of those they governed—those who were not warriors and priests. They denied education—reading, writing, arithmetic—to everyone but themselves. As a result, the Brahmins became learned but Sanskrit disappeared as a spoken language. New modes of writing and speaking emerged among the common people.

Sanskrit persisted, however, as the written language of Indian scholars and priests. It became the language in which the great body of Indian literature was composed. The most common form of written Sanskrit since c. 1000 A.D. is the Devanagari alphabet or "writing of the Gods," the number signs of which appear on the following pages (54–55). These numbers, like our modern numerals, are derived from the more ancient Brahmi script (see pages 20–23), in which Sanskrit had previously been recorded.

Used chiefly to express the holiness of the Hindu religion, Devanagari Sanskrit, nevertheless, influenced the design of more secular letters and numbers comprising the alphabets of other Asiatic lands.

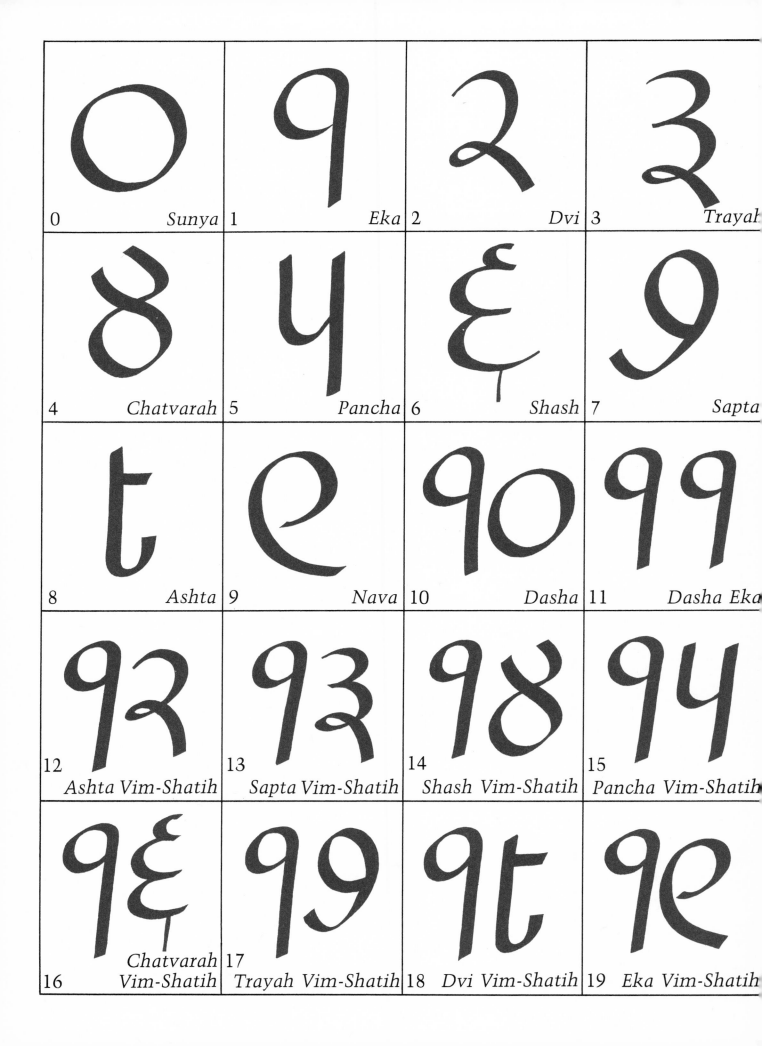

0 *Sunya*	1 *Eka*	2 *Dvi*	3 *Trayah*
4 *Chatvarah*	5 *Pancha*	6 *Shash*	7 *Sapta*
8 *Ashta*	9 *Nava*	10 *Dasha*	11 *Dasha Eka*
12 *Ashta Vim-Shatih*	13 *Sapta Vim-Shatih*	14 *Shash Vim-Shatih*	15 *Pancha Vim-Shatih*
16 *Chatvarah Vim-Shatih*	17 *Trayah Vim-Shatih*	18 *Dvi Vim-Shatih*	19 *Eka Vim-Shatih*

20 *Vim-Shatih*	21 *Nava Trim-Sat*	22 *Ashta TrimSat*	23 *Sapta Trim-Sat*
30 *Trim-Sat*	40 *Chatvarim-Sat*	50 *Pancha-Sat*	60 *Shash-Tih*
70 *Saptah-Sat*	80 *Ashi-Sat*	90 *Nava-Sat*	100 *Shatam*
200 *Dvi-Shatam*	300 *Tri-Shatam*	400 *Chatvarah-Shatam*	500 *Pancha-Shatam*
600 *Shash-Shatam*	700 *Sapta-Shatam*	800 *Ashta-Shatam*	900 *Nava-Shatam*

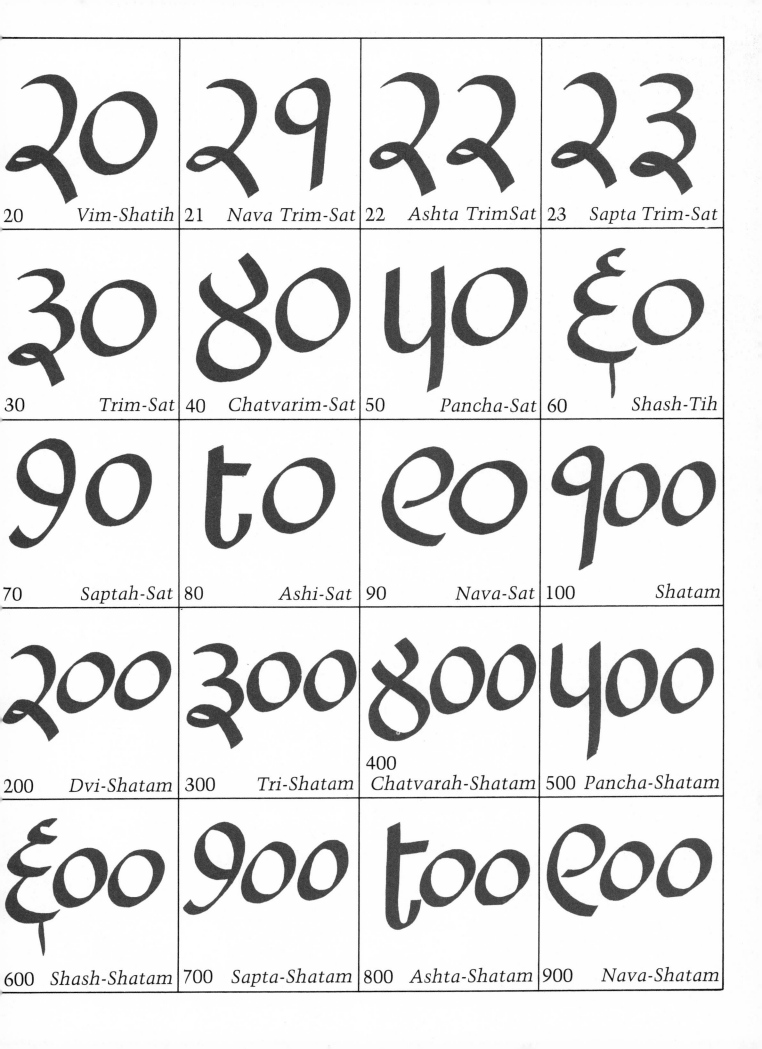

THAI

The history of modern Thailand began during the fourteenth century A.D. when Ayuthia was founded as the capital city of a fertile river valley comprising the Kingdom of Siam. Not much is known about the land and its people until then. For more than a thousand years a steady stream of Mongol tribes from central Asia had crossed the northern mountains, penetrated the tiger-ridden jungles, and filtered into the river valley further south. There, calling themselves Thais, they came into contact with Indian missionaries who converted them to Buddhism and introduced them to the Sanskrit alphabet and numbering system.

Eventually, these Thais formed city-states and fought with one another over control of the area. Finally, about 1350 A.D., they were welded into a single Siamese kingdom and faced more common enemies, the Burmese, Cambodians, and Laotians. By this time, the Siamese or Thais had adapted the Sanskrit alphabet with its numerical symbols to suit their own language needs as seen on pages 52–55.

Between 1500 and 1700, a succession of Portuguese, British, Dutch, and French trading vessels had opened the country to European interests. But the wars continued. By 1782, Ayuthia had been destroyed and a new capital, Bangkok, had been established by King Rama I. It was Rama's great grandson, King Rama IV, who modernized the country during the 1850s and who was the subject of the stage play and film *The King and I*, based on Margaret Landon's book *Anna and the King of Siam*.

In any event, Siam became Thailand just before World War II. And the country which had known constant turmoil during its long history continues to seethe with unrest as it approaches the twenty-first century.

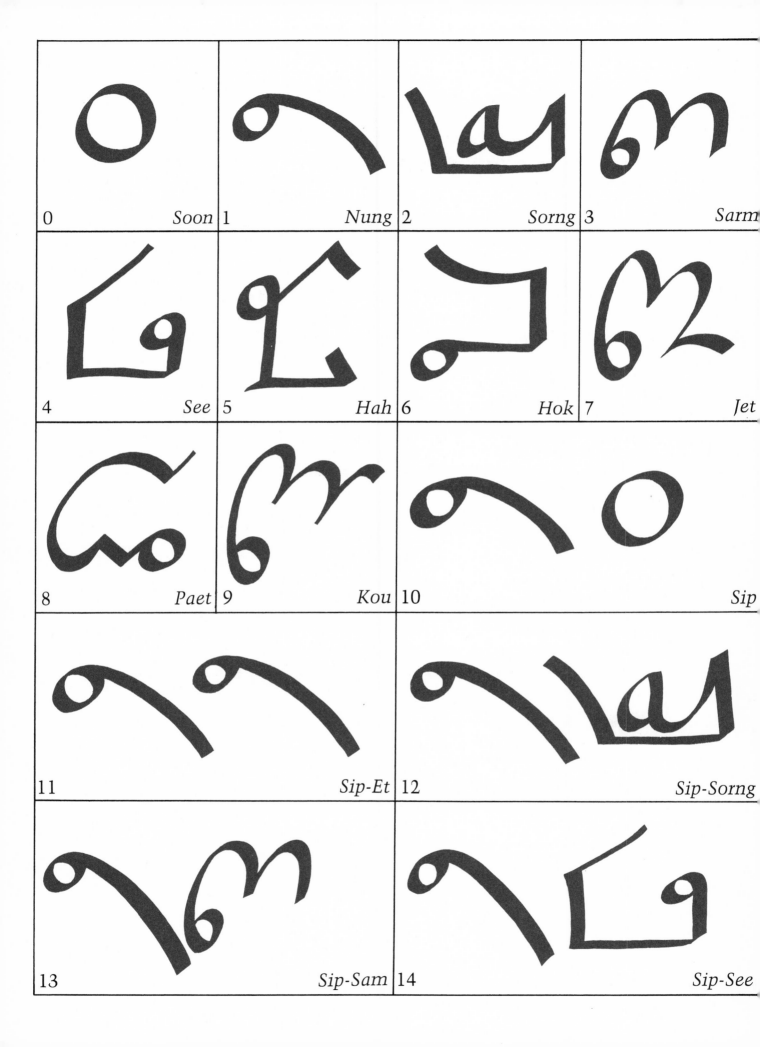

0 *Soon*	1 *Nung*	2 *Sorng*	3 *Sarm*
4 *See*	5 *Hah*	6 *Hok*	7 *Jet*
8 *Paet*	9 *Kou*	10 *Sip*	
11 *Sip-Et*	12 *Sip-Sorng*		
13 *Sip-Sam*	14 *Sip-See*		

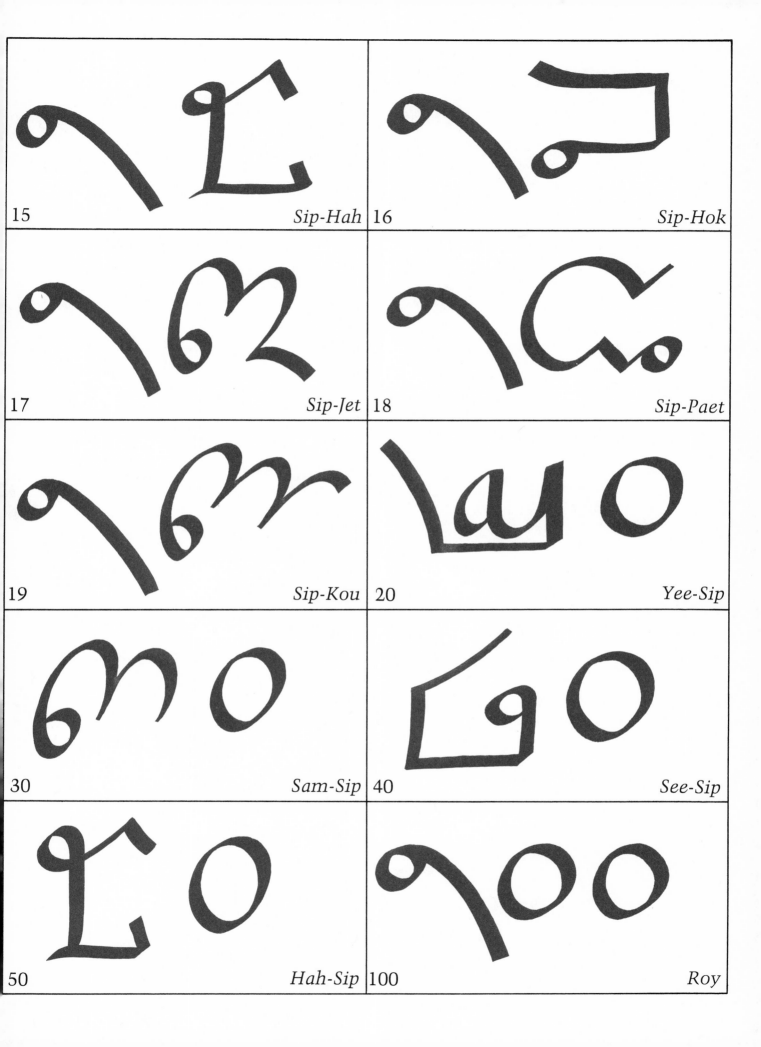

| 15 | *Sip-Hah* | 16 | *Sip-Hok* |

| 17 | *Sip-Jet* | 18 | *Sip-Paet* |

| 19 | *Sip-Kou* | 20 | *Yee-Sip* |

| 30 | *Sam-Sip* | 40 | *See-Sip* |

| 50 | *Hah-Sip* | 100 | *Roy* |

TIBETAN

Rising some 15,000 feet above sea level and ringed by the tallest mountains on earth, Tibet sits in lonely, windy isolation. The country is too cold to produce much more than barley; too barren to host a variant wildlife other than hairy yaks, sheep, and goats; and its rich deposits of gold, iron, and coal are nearly too inaccessible to mine. Tibet occupies the "roof of the world," while its 1,500,000 inhabitants, the "hermit people"—275,000 of whom are lamas or monks—huddle along the foothills enduring the howling storms and blizzards.

Travelers from India brought Buddhism and Sanskrit writing to Tibetan shepherds, farmers, and herdsmen at a time when the Middle Ages was bringing a new order to European society following the end of the Roman Empire (476 A.D.). Lhasa, the capital city, was founded during the 600s A.D. The Lhasan dialect became the *lingua franca*—the common language—among a people who spoke more than a hundred different dialects.

As the Middle Ages waned in Europe, Mongol hordes invaded Tibet imposing northern influences on Tibetan language and writing. By the 1600s the Dalai Lama had become the civil ruler while the Panchen Lama became the country's spiritual leader. Between 1720 and 1913, Tibet belonged to China. After that and for the next thirty-eight years, Tibet enjoyed independence. But Tibetan independence came to an end in 1951, when the People's Republic of China reestablished its rule.

The numerals appearing on the following pages are the commonly used numerals that predominated in Tibet as late as the first decade of the twentieth century. But like elsewhere in the world, these ordinary Tibetan numerals have been slowly giving way to the more standardized western Arabic numerals.

61

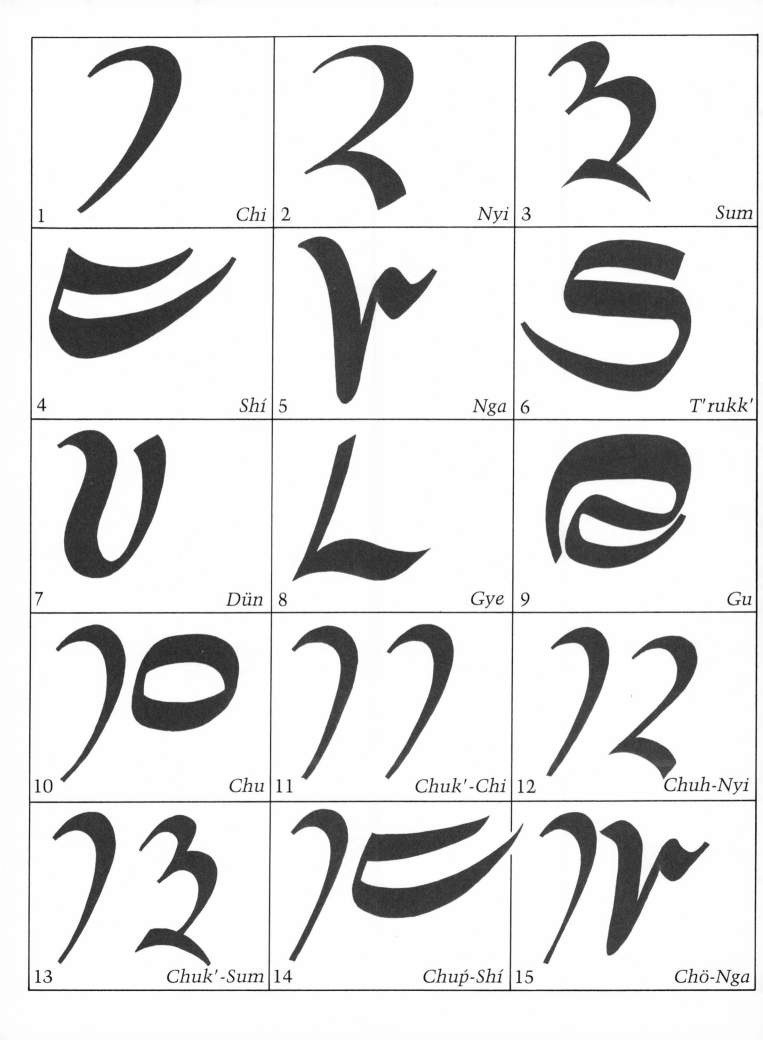

1 *Chi*	2 *Nyi*	3 *Sum*
4 *Shí*	5 *Nga*	6 *T'rukk'*
7 *Dün*	8 *Gye*	9 *Gu*
10 *Chu*	11 *Chuk'-Chi*	12 *Chuh-Nyi*
13 *Chuk'-Sum*	14 *Chup-Shí*	15 *Chö-Nga*

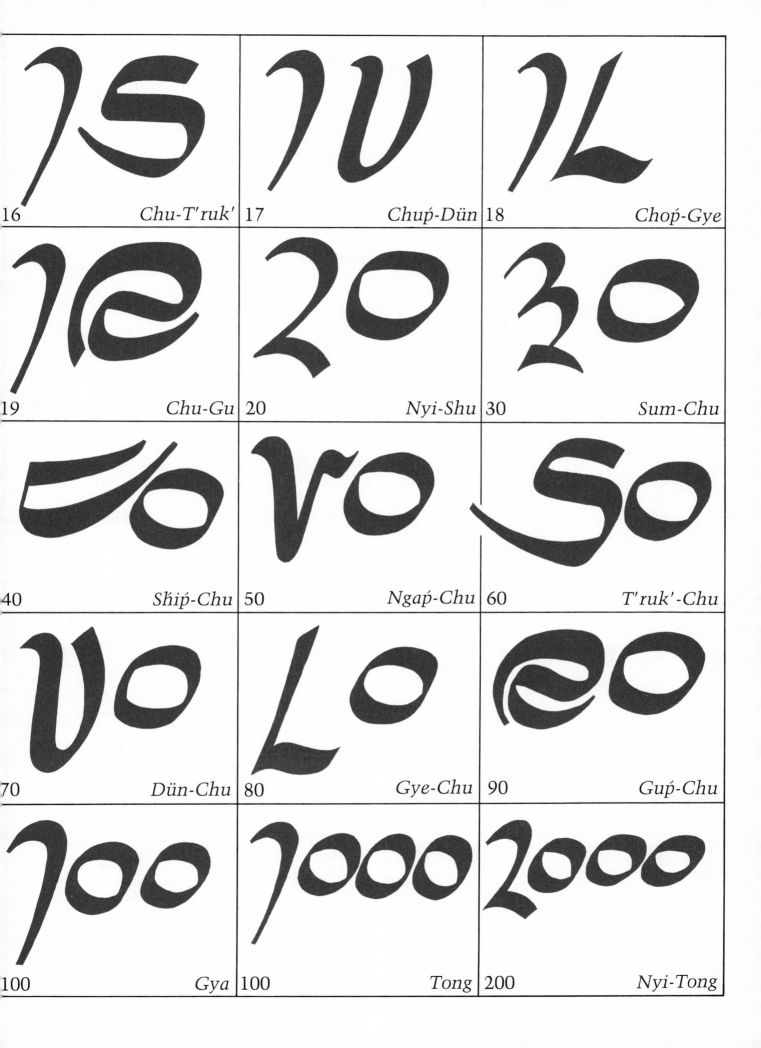

16 *Chu-T'ruk'*	17 *Chup-Dün*	18 *Chop-Gye*
19 *Chu-Gu*	20 *Nyi-Shu*	30 *Sum-Chu*
40 *Ship-Chu*	50 *Ngap-Chu*	60 *T'ruk'-Chu*
70 *Dün-Chu*	80 *Gye-Chu*	90 *Gup-Chu*
100 *Gya*	100 *Tong*	200 *Nyi-Tong*

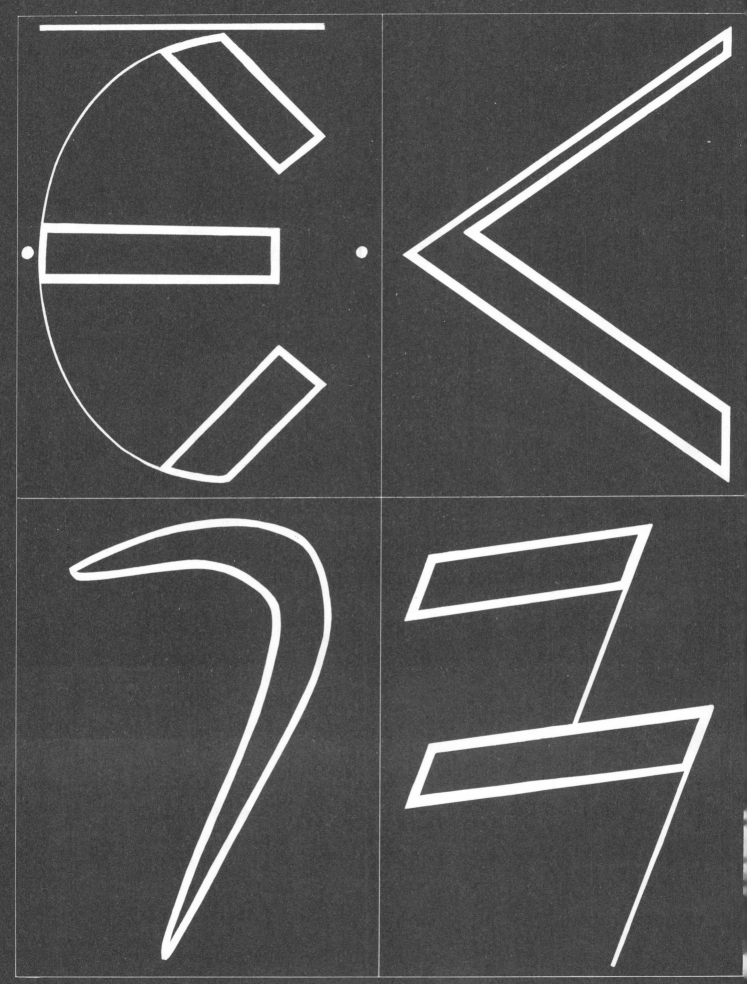

upper left: Gothic; *Upper right:* Runes; *lower left:* Brahmi; *lower right:* Egyptian